How do I use

Key Words with Peter and Ja[ne] parallel series, each containing twe[lve] [thr]ee series are written using the same [c] [] vocabulary. Readers will get the most out of **Key Words** with Peter and Jane when they follow the books in the pattern 1a, 1b, 1c; 2a, 2b, 2c and so on.

gradually introd[uces]

provides further p[ractice] in a different conte[xt]

• **Series c**
uses familiar words to teach **phonics** in a methodical way, enabling children to read increasingly difficult words. It also provides a link to writing.

Published by Ladybird Books Ltd
A Penguin Company
Penguin Books Ltd., 80 Strand, London WC2R 0RL, UK
Penguin Books Australia Ltd, 707 Collins Street, Melbourne, Victoria 3008, Australia
Penguin Group (NZ) 67 Apollo Drive, Rosedale, North Shore 0632, New Zealand

036

ISBN: 978-1-40930-112-7

Printed in China

Key Words

with Peter and Jane

2a

We have fun

written by W. Murray
illustrated by J.H. Wingfield

Here is Peter
and here is Jane.

Here is Pat, the dog.

new word

Pat

Peter is here.

Jane is here
and Pat is here.

Here they are.

new words

they   are

Here they are
in the water.

They like the water.

Pat likes the water.

Pat likes fun.

---

new words

water   fun

Come in, Pat.

It is fun.

It is fun in the water.

Come in the water.

Come, come, come.

---

new words

come   It   it

Pat comes in.

Pat likes the water.

It is fun in the water,
says Peter.

---

new word

says

I have a ball, says Peter

Here is the ball.

Here is the ball, Pat,
he says.

---

new words

have   he

Look, look, says Jane.

Look, Peter, look.

Have a look.

Come and look.

Peter has a look.

---

new word

Look   look

Peter looks.

A fish, says Jane.

It is a fish, says Peter.

It is a fish, he says.

---

new word

fish

Look, says Peter.

The dog wants the fish.

He wants the fish, Jane.

---

new word

wants

Pat wants the fish.

No, no, no, says Jane,
you come here.

Come here, Pat, come here

No, no, no.

new words

No   no   you

Here are Peter and Jane

Peter has some water.

Here you are, Jane,
he says.

---

new word

some

Here you are, Jane, says Peter.

Here you are.

This is for you.

Here is some water for you.

---

new words

for   This   this

This is for you, Jane say.

Here is some water
for you.

Here you are, Peter.

It is for you.

no new words

Look Jane, I can jump,
says Peter.

I can jump in the water.

Can you jump
like this, Jane?

---

new words

can   jump

Jane can jump
and Peter can jump.

They jump into the wate
for fun.

We like this, they say.

---

new words

      into We we

Jump this, Pat, jump this
says Peter.

Jump in the water.

You can jump.

Pat jumps into the water

no new words

Pat jumps.

He jumps into the water

He likes to jump.

It is fun, says Jane,
we like this.

---

new word

to

We have to go, says Peter

Come, Jane.
Come, he says.
We have to go.

new word

go

We have to go, Pat,
says Jane.
Come, Pat, come.

Yes, says Peter,
we have to go.

---

new word

Yes   yes

Can we have some sweets
says Jane.

Can we go to the shop
for some sweets ?

Yes, says Peter.

---

new word

sweets

This is the shop, Jane.

Yes, this is it.

They have sweets and toy

We want sweets, says Jan

Peter and Jane go into the sweet shop.

Pat is in the shop.

Jane and Peter have some sweets.

Pat has a sweet.

---

no new words

I want to go home,
says Jane.

Yes, I want to go home,
says Peter.

Come, Pat, come.

We want to go home.

---

new word

home

Here we are, says Jane.
We are home.
It is fun in the water.

Yes, says Peter,
we have fun in the water.

New words used in this book

Total number of new words: 27
Average repetition per word: 10